Everything Moves with a Disfigured Grace

For more information visit www.alsopreview.com

Design & Typography by Robt. Ward

ISBN 0-9761954-2-9

Orders, enquiries, and correspondence should be addressed to:

Alsop Review, Ltd.
122 Broad Creek Road,
Laurel, DE 19956

Everything Moves with a Disfigured Grace

Selected Poems

• Robert Lavett Smith •

The Alsop Review Press

Acknowledgments

Some of these poems first appeared in the following periodicals, to whom grateful acknowledgment is given:

Anthology One (The Alsop Review): "Don't Look Now"

Blue Unicorn: "Ciro on the Night Before his Wedding"

Curriculum Vitae: "My Grandfather's Vigil"

The Distillery: "Walking Across the Sea of Galilee" (in an earlier version)

The Eckerd College Review: "The Nuns' Madhouse"

Footprints Magazine: "The Clockwork Farm" (in an earlier version)

The Higginsville Reader: "Sunrise, San Francisco, September 1, 1999"

The High Plains Literary Review: "The Dolls"

Illya's Honey: "Landscape With Figure, Standing Apart"

Mind Purge: "Maxfield Parrish"

Mudfish: "Electrocuting The Elephant" (in an earlier version)

The New Laurel Review: "The Trouble with the Garage Sale"

The New Now Now New Millennium Turn-On Anthology: "Droppings"; "Night Braces"; "The Onset of Something Ominous"; "The Ordinary Arrival of Death"

Plainsongs: "The Skull of Billy The Kid"

Pudding Magazine: "Gardening Along the Fire Scars: Oakland, 1993"

The Raintown Review: "Catechism for a Leper" (in an earlier version)

Red Owl Magazine: "The Ceremony"

Touchstone: "The Partial Hospitalization Unit"

Octavo: "Dustbowl Funeral"

Publication of this book has been made possible, in part,
by a gift in memory of Phyllis J. Guth.

Dedication

For Pat, with all my love:

"Every heart
to love will come
but like a refugee."

—Leonard Cohen

Patricia Lewis Smith, 1953-2005

The Alsop Review Press

Contents

Part 1: Don't Look Now

Part 2: The Onset of Something Ominous

Part 3: The Ordinary Arrival of Death

Part 1: Don't Look Now

The Skull Of Billy The Kid

> *"Three months after the Kid's death, a Montana newspaper reported that his body had been dug up, his head removed, and the skull polished in a manner appropriate to a relic."*
> *—from an article in* **The New Yorker**

Outlaw or not, William Bonney was a devout
Presbyterian and a former Irish Catholic
whose death elicited the usual dreary hymns.
Candles surrounded his grieving mother
like gun barrels aimed towards heaven.

Shot in the desert, miles from anywhere
last rites could be said for his soul, his body
grayed with the dust which would reclaim him.
And after his death the halo of his youth
and exploits burned ever more brightly.

But this other story interests me, the skull,
stolen by nameless admirers, rubbed until
it shone like onyx. His wanderlust outliving him
as it toured the West in some snake-oil show,
nestled in cheap velvet, five cents to see.

Why disturb its dark sleep? Murderer,
martyr, sinner or saint, Billy belongs to history now,
where the dead are restless, and never wholly themselves.

I can almost feel its weight in my hands,
the cracked surface cool and smooth, brown as a stone.
The pooled sockets which held his eyes regarding me
without apology, as if surprised to be here,
on the threshold of yet another century.

The Final Hours Of The Twentieth Century

A few strands of cloud
dyed pink by the last
of the sunset, above
a street of tenements
where the lights
are just beginning
to come on.
And the sky,
a turgid water—
where the first stars appear
like flotsam after a shipwreck.

San Francisco, December 31, 2000

From One Who Has No Right To Grieve

In memoriam: G. William Lewis, 1923-1998

Late afternoon. We sit by the window,
in the house you built with your own hands
when you were the man who held his smiling bride
in the photographs fading all around us.

Your eyes are heavy, nearly opaque.
The Bay is flat and bright as steel,
the hills above us luminous
against the threatening sky.

"Looks like rain," you manage to say
before sinking back into the sleep
which seldom releases you now,
struggling under its dark weight.

An order of service lies on the coffee table,
left behind by the deacons who came earlier
to give you communion, its white pages spread
on the dim wood like the promise of heaven.

But I'd rather pray for those
who must remain here without you.

When you are gone—soon—I'll have
no right to grieve, for I barely know you;
I'll marry your daughter at a wedding
we both know you won't attend.
I promise to love and treat her well.

And I promise always to remember you,
the way each gesture apologizes for who
you no longer are. "Strong," you insisted
when we first met, "I used to be strong."

My Grandfather's Vigil

In memoriam: Dr. Walter E. Maple, 1899-1968

In all my memories of him it's early evening,
dust-furred sunlight spilling through lace curtains
in the bay window. He's crumpled in the high
burgundy armchair, a gaunt, gasping silhouette.

The veins in his forehead are roots,
tiny and blue beneath translucent skin;
his hair by now is white, thinned
until nothing remains of it but light.

His head's thrown back, eyes closed, mouth open;
he struggles even in sleep to haul coarse ropes of air
into lungs already ruined by emphysema. Barely six,
I know instinctively he hasn't got much longer to live.

A rifle from the basement cabinet rests on his knees,
its oiled barrel gleaming as night falls. He's slept with it
for years, no explanations, won't be dissuaded. He rages
at any who dare suggest that this is, at best, foolishness.

My grandmother's hidden the cache of bullets he made
by hand at his forge in the shed, buried his gunpowder
with the beans and summer squash. Still, there are rumors
in the neighborhood, whispers in the pews on Sunday.

Of course I won't know that for years. For now, somehow,
it doesn't seem strange to be playing here on the carpet at his feet,
admiring his gun, the bloodless knuckles of his hands, and in the
window behind him, the star-gnawed sky darkening above the elms.

The Clockwork Farm

Insert a quarter, and tiny carvings
spring to life. A yellowed sky
encloses it all; invisible gears
animate a scene excessively quaint,
unreal even to those who built it.

I remember the rough country of pain,
a wilderness of crutches, braces and canes.

The awkward dance of those days
is mirrored in these dusty miniatures,
bound by an awful gravity through which
everything moves with a disfigured grace.

Landscape With Figure, Standing Apart

Behind houses where streetlights
are just now beginning to flicker,
the lake deepens into twilight:
nearly invisible through pale trees,
its shadowy waters sharp with stars.

The first soft rustle of evening spreads,
becoming something not quite a stillness.

One by one, windows blink on
like dreamers roused from sleep;
silhouettes quiver behind bright curtains.
But the blind eye of the rising moon
reminds me I haven't come to stay.

Already they study one another shyly,
anticipating passions I won't share.
Only hours from now, on dozens of streets,
in hundreds of identical rooms, clothes will fall gently
from aging limbs, and from the astonished bodies
of those first discovering love.

I consider it all with a kind of nostalgia,
the way a patient recovering from amnesia
looks back with surprising tenderness
at the blizzard receding in his head.

Bearing the darkness before me
like a lantern, I move on.

Deaf Woman Wrapping Christmas Gifts At Borders

She cannot hear
the tiny, elastic sound
of cellophane tape
being torn from the dispenser,
the minute crackle
of the wrapping paper
her quick fingers crease
and fold expertly over,
nor the infinitely small
kisses her fingertips make
against the tense drum
of the shrink wrap
enclosing a CD—
this thing which is, itself,
the palpable manifestation
of what she cannot miss,
never having known it;
what she cannot imagine
even as it enfolds her,
as present and unnoticed as the air.

Dustbowl Funeral

for James Weddington

Near dawn, the farm hands dressed by candlelight,
their hair tonic thick, and rank with kerosene.
They fixed stiff collars to their starched white shirts,
and rinsed their mouths with urine to sweeten their breath.

They dressed in black, in suits they knew they'd wear
when, one day, they were laid in their own graves.
Such finery as they possessed was grayed
by the dust that covered everything like despair.

Dust storms had scoured the whitewash from the walls
of the clapboard church across the barren fields.
They walked together in silence, knowing the way;
in silence, after the service, they carried the coffin.

Six mourners bore that body through a landscape
as still and colorless as a photograph;
the only sound besides their own footsteps,
dust devils howling through abandoned farms.

The dry husks of dead locusts were impaled
on barbed wire fences: many thousands of them,
so that the wires sagged beneath the weight
like branches burdened with some hideous fruit.

Gardening Along The Fire Scars: Oakland, 1993

for Larry Conrad

Beneath the hissing of the hose
the compost pile smolders under fig trees.
"That's cooking nicely," you say, and I smile,
pleased with the metaphor. But you mean it,
grinning as you remove your heavy gloves,
determined to prove the thing's on fire.

And so it is, exactly as you claim.
When we reach into the mulch's hairy flanks,
it's hot inside, like reaching into a living thing:
a handful of dead leaves is moist and heavy,
as I imagine a beating heart might be
were one somehow to hold it.

Across the ridge, where the ground is barren,
they're rebuilding from the blaze two summers ago.
Rising through fireweed, skeleton houses
blacken against the conflagration of sunset.

As the first stars sharpen on the horizon,
we stand in the softly breathing yard, among
the darkening smells of mown grass and twilight,
wrapped in the world's slow, steady burning.

Don’t Look Now

Somewhere above us,
gargoyles cough in their gutters.
Library lions yawn and lick their paws.
In formal gardens, sundials
lean discreetly towards the light,
pliant as heliotrope.
The mirror admires
its own reflection.
Scissors dream
of a whetstone’s kiss,
opening and closing
gently in their sleep.
If you listen, you can hear
the asthmatic rasp of the wine.

In The Name Of Science

In memory of Marjorie Ransom, who told me this story

This death is quietly awful in its immensity.
Near sunset, a mountain of gasping flesh
struggles into the shallows, then gives up.

It's a humpback who's strayed too close
to shore, stranded by the retreating tide.
Flanks bright as glass at first, then swollen,
cracking in the stale air, starting to stink
beneath a glittering cloud of flies.

Soon men from town arrive, furred beams
of headlights quivering along the surf line,
thinning to nothing before the ocean's
endless emptiness. They've brought ropes
and tackles, saws honed to pure cold light.

But who are these two tiny figures
astride the whale's barnacled back
shouting obscenities in pantomime,
gesturing wildly to the roaring night?

For years the locals will tell anyone who'll listen
about the time the biologists fought over a flayed humpback.
Laid bare by their tools, entirely indifferent to argument,
the disputed organs gleam wetly in the moonlight.
The liver bloated with the dampness of decay,
the stilled heart enshrined in its vault of ribs,
the lungs like sails becalmed in the briny darkness.

After Brain Surgery

Eight weeks in coma, endlessly adrift
atop the blue inflated mattress meant
to stop your skin's erupting into sores.

Beneath the monitor's insistent scrawl
the dim moons of your eyes turn from the sun,
blindly pursuing orbits of their own,
shackled to sleep's interior gravity.

Your parted lips are working wordlessly
around the swollen silence of your tongue.

The dumb obedient sprouting of your hair
from your shorn scalp amounts to nothing more
than the body's reassertion of dull need.

If only I were sure your twitching eyes
were more than random electricity,
I might not feel your absence quite so keenly—
the sheer brute force of it against my world.

Classical Musicians In The Subway

"Tant pis pour le bois qui se trouve violon."
—Arthur Rimbaud

There's a sadness in even the most jubilant music,
a hint of death. Consider, for instance, the rosined
horsehair in the violinist's bow, which slides so easily
across the lengths of tightened catgut, drawing out
that brief, exquisite cry of perfect pain
which we call *art* because to name it truly
would be to recognize the murder in it:
the violin, the cello once were trees,
green, growing things whose leaves
sang the subtler songs of the wind.
Yet the beauty of music is that it perishes,
each individual note a moment in time,
the melody discernible only as memory.
Not that that matters in this airless place
where multitudes rush blindly through the dark...

Kickballs

Even now, at the start of a new century,
they're identical to the ones we chased
across the asphalt schoolyards of the '60s
while our older brothers fell in Vietnam
and Kennedy, in flickering black and white,
promised Americans we'd reach the moon—
the moon, which was itself a yellow kickball
some kid's well-planted foot had sent sailing
over the backstop, beyond the cyclone fence.

Brie And Chianti At Midnight

In a tiny hotel room in a city renowned
for its medieval bridges, we share quiet
caresses, brie and Chianti at midnight.

We have learned silence on our
journey together, passing through
lands where our words were useless.

My eager hands navigate your face
in the darkness: an oddly joyous act,
like reading a Bach sonata in Braille.

At Last, Like Sleepers

At last, like sleepers timidly emerging
from dreams of blindness, we awake to love,
finding our once-familiar lives transformed:
well-trodden paths lead to strange destinations,
and books we knew by heart delight anew
with passages we've never read before.

The light that fills our world is no longer
confined to wavelengths visible to the eye;
instead, it seems to rise from deep inside,
a radiance not so much observed, as *felt.*
No color on the palette quite describes it;
no words we know are equal to the task.

Bob Dylan Is Stopped By His Own Security

"Even if they knew who Dylan was, the guards had strict orders that no one was to get backstage without an official credential."
—from a newspaper report, November, 2001

One can imagine the ice in his blue eyes
as they narrow to appraise these young upstarts
whose tattooed arms are folded across their chests
in a posture suggesting they will not be moved.

Beneath a wispy mustache, his lips curl
into a sneer resembling the one
with which a youthful version of himself
peered warily from the sleeve of his first album.

Four decades since have creased his weathered face,
hollowed his once-round cheeks until they seem
as ancient as the endless roads he's traveled:
now he looks older than his sixty years.

Yet—for so small a man—he carries himself
with an enormous dignity, that suggests
the poise of Big Joe Williams or Lightnin' Hopkins,
earned from a life steeped in the Delta Blues.

He stares the shaven-headed giants down
without a word, his silence withering.
Unnerved, they step aside to let him pass,
trailing the weight of history in his wake.

The Trouble With The Garage Sale

Nothing has readied me
for such bottomless hunger.
Geriatric Russians,
frail and white,
arrive by the dozens:
so wraith-like and fragile
light seems to fall through them.

They're tougher than they look.
Gesturing madly with canes,
they spill from garage
to unguarded apartment:
a hydra of grasping hands,
gibbering as if possessed;
tearing down pictures, looting
closets, ripping out the phone.

(I know whatever nights
are left here will be gnawed
by dreams of appalling need;
moonrises swollen with leering,
translucent faces: aged grotesques,
finely veined masks of pure greed.)

And it goes on. A red-faced man
whose breath is rank with vodka
astonishes me by insisting he'll buy
my unpaid phone bill, mislaid on a table.

In minutes only hooks and bare walls remain.
These, and my cash box, still woefully empty.
Over my protests, hulking matrons load
dirty dishes from the sink into huge purses.

Dreaming In Black And White

I live alone in a desolate neighborhood,
a world delineated in shades of dirty gray.
The mechanical whine of an ancient elevator
troubles my sleep; sweating through steam heat,
I leave my window open on even the coldest evenings.

It's like an old joke whose punch line's forgotten.
On the corner, Latino drag queens smoke,
idly swing purses, adjust padded bras.
Their eyes drift on the darkness of makeup;
veins swell horribly on their thin arms.

I observe life with the dispassionate eye
of a journalist's camera recording a massacre.
I sleep poorly, can barely imagine sex;
if I ever loved, I don't recall it now.

What spirituality endures here
emanates from a storefront church,
once a movie theater, half a block away:
the marquee proclaims all are welcome;
the letters are askew, unevenly lit from above,
where the assurance that *Jesus Saves* is tattooed
in flickering neon on a dense, immobile sky.

Nightly, in the littered street, sirens rush
towards disasters that don't concern me;
an old woman screams at no one in particular,
screams and screams in the endless drizzle.

San Francisco, Good Friday, 1995

Etta And The Seagulls

Etta James, performing within sight
of the Golden Gate, on an outdoor stage
at the San Francisco Blues Festival,
lets loose a series of shrieks
and animal groans from deep in the jungle
of her great heart, drums and upright
bass keeping time behind something
older, more essential, than words.

And suddenly an enormous spiraling cloud
of seagulls descends from a clear sky.
White wings quivering with sunlight,
they tattoo the air with their answering cries.

Little Elegy

In memoriam: Vassar Miller, American poet, 1924-1998

Let us go down
to the stark Eden
of our deaths, that
grim paradise,
having truly lived.

May the wind in our bones
recognize the place,
asking nothing of God
but the chance to rest
there awhile; perhaps
just long enough
to remember you.

Part 2: The Onset of Something Ominous

Chinese New Year, The Bowery

for Raymond Shen

Sometimes I can still see the dragon's
sequined, snapping jaws, the pale ribbon
of his body winding through swarming streets
where the dancers' footprints turn to smoke.

We kneel on a littered stoop, loading our cameras;
the smell of gunpowder clings to our hair and clothes.
A blizzard of burnt paper drifts over dreaming winos,
shopkeepers setting out spices for the bodiless dead.

Crossing Larkspur Ferry

"Flood-tide below me! I see you face to face!"
—Walt Whitman

Kneeling beside me, Mark tries in vain
to light a cigarette in strong wind, pointedly
ignoring the *No Smoking* sign posted nearby;
cursing under his breath as the flame goes out.

We rumble past Alcatraz, where birds nest
in the abandoned guard towers; past Angel
Island's unpeopled flanks; past the Marin
Headlands, already darkly mantled in mist.

Everything stands out sharply, as it does in dreams;
the light is what a friend in New York would call
mescaline light. Mark begins to reminisce about
Back East, where they have four distinct seasons.

He remembers when the Staten Island Ferry
was a "cheap date"; how twenty years ago,
he and Danny Ratcliff used to take their girls
out on the water, drunk on salt air and beer.

A little sadly, I realize we're no longer young—
somehow surprised by knowledge I bear daily now.
Times like these, when the weather's nearly perfect,
are rarer than they were; there's no doubt about it.

Nowadays, my life *weighs more* than it once did.
Something is bearing down on me, with a force
I'm helpless to resist. Mark feels it too, I know;
it passes unsaid between us, needing no words.

Rounding the point where San Quentin broods
like a medieval nightmare, we watch windsurfers
darting like dragonflies through the vessel's wake,
their transparent sails ethereal in a haze of spray.

One of them topples and goes down;
I think how we're always treading water,
every one of us, every day of our lives,
swept seaward by currents we can't control.

Night Braces

"Pain comes from the darkness,
And we call it wisdom. It is pain."
—Randall Jarrell

Adrift in the darkness of my fortieth year,
I feel again the heavy leather shoes
my father laced me into when I was four,
the way the gleaming metal braces
clicked into sockets in the heels.

How I cried out as he tightened the straps
that encircled each leg just below the knee,
until they blazed their angry alphabet into my skin,
years before the surgery would leave its scars.

Long after his footsteps faded
the glass of water he left behind
glowed on the nightstand, lit
by a luminous shroud of sky
in the bedroom window.

Then I could feel a groan too faint for the ear,
the slow creak of tendons tightening on bone.

The stillness was broken twice an hour
by the mechanical cry of the cuckoo,
and sometimes by some farther bird
in whose inhuman trill I knew already
the harsh economy of pain.

The Cathedral

On the walk from the station,
heat climbs like smoke from empty plazas.
At the youth hostel, there are no vacancies.
I meet an Irishman named Ivan; ten dollars
between us, we decide to share a room nearby.

Ivan drinks red wine all night, talking loudly
about girls he's laid all across Europe.
By bad light, I eat a blood orange,
wrapping the rest in newspaper.

Before dawn, we set out
for the hill above town,
machine gun fire only blocks away.
The bus is packed with old women in black,
live chickens in wicker baskets.
It wobbles unsteadily down steep inclines,
narrow streets lined with shuttered houses.
Gaudi's unfinished masterpiece soars
like a drunken dream into a luminous sky.

In the roofless nave, the sun, already blistering,
beats down on columns like enormous trees.
Ivan takes a swig from a barely concealed bottle,
laughing wildly, his dark hair
flickering in the burning breeze.
Gargoyles leer from the parapets.
A cloud of dusty pigeons rises
through the empty rose window,
a host of derelict angels.

Barcelona, Summer, 1977

The Partial Hospitalization Unit

"I am, yet what I am, none cares or knows..."
—John Clare

In the library I unearth Sandburg's *Remembrance Rock*,
an anthology listing Yeats as a living poet, *Hungarian Cooking*.
Ours is an open ward, fairly quiet. But on the way to the restroom,
one must pass Intensive Care, its heavy steel door barred like a vault.
I can see nothing through the narrow window; I often hear screams,
sometimes sobbing—once, a sort of scraping sound I can't identify.

I do not sleep here. Every morning I arrive by streetcar.
On Mondays, we fill out lunch menus for the week.
It's always the same choices; the food, at least, is good.
None of the other patients speak as we unload our trays.
Usually, we eat in silence. The thin Salvadorian weeps softly.

For group therapy we arrange ourselves in a circle.
The social worker sits among us: plain, prim dress,
tight hair. Today the lesbian tells in a flinty voice
how her parents disowned her when she came out.
She doesn't like me, but nods when the Chinese kid
says he's been unable to leave his room for weeks.
Two hundred milligrams of *Zoloft* do nothing
to ease my growing sense of hopelessness.

Private sessions are even worse. When I tell the smug,
indifferent doctor in his tweed vest I'm still angry at a woman
who wrongfully accused me of harassment, his eyes narrow.
Do I know of the Terasoff Mandate, that he's required to warn
anyone I might intend to hurt? I insist I'm not violent,
but he isn't listening. He asks if I'm calmer on medication.
There's no point in bothering to answer.

Langley Porter Psychiatric Hospital, San Francisco, 1996

The Onset Of Something Ominous

Late afternoon, and the Pacific's a sheet
of burning metal wrinkling against the shore.
I stand for hours on the embankment
watching the sinking sun unraveling on the water.

Thoughts splinter like light among the froth and kelp.
Growing up with each step and gesture a struggle
hardens one too much to permit illusions: it isn't lust
or pity I wrestle with, but an encroaching grimness.

I'm thinking of a woman with Chinese writing
tattooed on the skin at the base of her neck.
I consider her now, not with longing,
but with something approaching despair.

High overhead, seagulls wheel
in torn circles through the twilight.
By the water's edge, the shadows
of the last birds shiver and take flight,
a flurry of wingbeats in the darkness.

I can still hear their departure
long after I no longer see them.
Night fills the emptiness they leave behind;
wind rattles the coarse grass of the dunes
as I turn and climb towards a sky without stars.

A Lament For My Forty-Fourth Year

"...lonely men in shirt-sleeves, leaning out of windows..."
—T. S. Eliot

Already I imagine
I can see the beginnings
of the one I will someday become.
Old men on street corners
watch me with clouded eyes—
their slack faces fading
like the faces of statues
blurred by years of rain,
the blue hair of veins
leaking like languor
through their papery skin.

Catechism For A Leper

> *"The officiating priest threw a handful of earth*
> *from the cemetery on the head of the leper three times,*
> *explaining that the ritual symbolizes the death*
> *of the leper to the world."*
> —*Saul Nathaniel Brody,* **The Disease of the Soul**

A Latin blessing trembles like the wind.
The priest explains the funeral is your own,
although for years to come you'll roam the world,
your eyes averted from the eyes of men,
your heavy footsteps like a tolling bell.

Feel the stench of graves anointing you:
decrepit earth, full of worm-stink and rot.
Know in your blindness that somewhere above,
the rose window is colorless and black,
empty at midnight as a gaping socket.

Attempt to concentrate on the only thing
you *can* see through the coarse cloth of your cowl:
the flames of candles on the distant altar,
cold and uncertain as the hope of heaven,
like burning tears of an abandoned god.

Rise quietly, and quickly cross yourself
as you depart, your hood swept from your eyes.
Stand in the mossy portico, among the saints,
the demons with their breasts of rain-dimmed stone,
their pity swallowed by the ravenous dark.

Then contemplate the road ahead of you:
a dusty torrent rushing towards a future
where Death awaits you with his arms outspread.
His emaciated body is your own:
a breathing corpse awash with running sores.

The Truest World

The truest world is a vicious one,
whose nonchalant brutality
we glimpse only occasionally,
in moments of insight
that freeze the blood.

Today, for instance: high above
the "Hawks" logo on the retaining wall
reinforcing the hillside behind the playground,
I saw a real hawk—a silent, breathing crucifix
floating effortlessly in the overcast sky.

Ciro On The Night Before His Wedding

I still remember his face,
younger than mine is now;
he sat in the flickering darkness,
arms folded on the steering wheel
of the tour bus, cigarette smoke
wreathing his head like a garnish
around the head of John the Baptist.

The marriage was arranged in the old way,
an alliance between families, a concept hard
for school kids from New Jersey to fathom:
he'd shrugged and told us (through an interpreter)
he didn't really know his future wife, had met her
once, maybe twice, didn't care, didn't really
think about it much one way or the other.

But I stayed behind while the others went
to climb the Spanish Steps, sitting with him
in the shadows, the idling engine tearing at silence,
no language flowering in the space between us.

I watched uneasily as composure was blown
from his features like dust from the surrounding ruins,
his dark eyes hardened by something more bitter
than sadness. We'd have another driver, I knew,
for the morning's trip south to the temples of Paestum.

Rome, 1975

The Nuns' Madhouse

"He heard a mad nun screaming
in the nuns' madhouse beyond the wall."
—James Joyce

Here where it always seems to be night
they gather, wild-eyed, veins twitching
in their pinched, translucent faces.

Nurses move quietly among them,
melancholy angels carrying bedpans,
vials of blood bright as votive candles.

Above, in shadow, the body of Jesus
hangs like a limp sail from the mast
of a crucifix becalmed on the wall.

The Ceremony

There was a sweet smoke rising.
Silently and according to custom,
they washed the hair in urine,
sewed ears and nostrils shut,
stuffed the mouth with spices.
They dressed the infant's corpse
in an elaborate wedding gown,
determined to marry her
to the dead son of a prominent family
that she might not be lonely in paradise—
their own unspeakable grief woven
like river grass into her nuptial shroud.

The moon hung swollen and red.
Over the tiny bride they kept a vigil,
the silence pierced now and then
by the thin howl of a starving dog.
Near dawn, the ancestors
gathered just beyond the firelight:
tall, muscular folk with no faces,
sweat shining on their perfect limbs,
only darkness where their eyes should be.

The Last Shakers Of Sabbathday Lake

"In the meetinghouse, we sit on plain benches. Walls are white, woodwork blue, the colors of light and sky."
—Richard and Joyce Wolkomir, "Living a Tradition,"
in **Smithsonian**, *April, 2001*

Only eight still remain
of a sect which numbered
in the hundreds a century ago:
four men, four women, who sit
piously in the calm blue interior
of the meetinghouse, reading
aloud from an ancient Bible.

Through simple windows,
light falls into the thin white
hair of their bowed heads,
the camera making it look
(we must suspect deliberately)
almost as if they are haloed.

What's haunting in the photo
is what one hopes will endure
when they are gone: the honesty
of this room whose straight lines
lend it a kind of resolute dignity,
and of the altar, adorned plainly
with nothing but a wooden
bowl of perfect sunflowers.

Nothing I Love Has Ever Seemed Permanent

for Pat

When I wake beside you the rags of summer sky
visible through partially drawn drapes are already
as thin and shimmering as blown glass. You're still
sleeping, sheets kicked away from your nakedness,
the curve of your shoulders traced faintly by the flicker
of the last streetlights. Propped on one elbow, I lie
watching for a long time as you curl more tightly into
some dream I can't share, smiling softly in your sleep.

At this hour loneliness is palpable even to lovers waking
in each other's arms. Across the way, by a cyclone fence,
the buses in the municipal yard doze in the intricate dark;
on the hill above them the neon sign over the storage facility,
partially burned out, prints the word *rage* in huge letters
on the waking world. The streets are wet, savagely quiet.

It's the most vulnerable time of day. Alone beside you here
in the fading shadows, I feel frail and old. There are some things
I fear: death, and the ordinary business of living. Nothing I love
has ever seemed permanent. I can scarce believe we're together
now, in this bed worn comfortable by the indentations of our bodies,
places where we fit gently into one another. Around us the new
day takes shape; the struggle begins. Frightened and joyous, let me
wake you with a kiss for luck, watching the rinsed light rise in your eyes.

Terrors Of The Millennium

> *"The pious were awaiting the coming of either the Redeemer or the Devil. The reason? The millennium was ending, and apocalypse seemed right around the corner."*
> —***Smithsonian**, July, 1999*

Somewhere in Wales—let's say—
it's the end of the twentieth century.
Swallows nest in a ruined priory
while thunderheads gather in empty
windows, their *vitreaux* broken
by Henry's men, perhaps, or simply
crushed under the weight of centuries.

Foxglove and thistle push aside
tiles where a thousand years ago
the faithful lay prostrate: throngs
of penitents naked and bleeding
from hideous mortifications;
exhausted at the millennial hour;
throats hymned to hoarseness.

Those days are a distant echo,
a subtle dance of shadows only.
Their bones will not speak now;
they are no longer even dust.

The rain which begins, heavily,
is not a portent, neither brimstone
nor blood: it is rain. It falls as it must
on the oblivious hills, as the autumn night
settles over the drenched green world.

Walking Across The Sea Of Galilee

The Israeli government has approved plans to build a barely-submerged foot bridge beneath the Sea of Galilee.

Our aging guide moves with surprising agility.
Ahead of me two Serbian nuns struggle to keep
their balance on the submerged path, the hems
of their habits already soaked, brilliantly white
running shoes showing under dark, heavy skirts.

On either side of the narrow span, lifeguard stations,
uncomfortable-looking straight-backed chairs bolted
to wooden rafts, sway on chains furred with algae,
like tiny islands anchored deep in opaque water.

The lifeguards listen to Berlioz on a transistor radio.
Machine guns lie across their knees, gleaming dully;
sunlight slides easily off their bare brown shoulders.

Though the land's nearly two miles distant,
the scorched hills sharpen in the morning light.
There are no railings. We must walk carefully,
gingerly, arms outspread like awkward wings.

Yet it's easy to believe in this manufactured miracle.
We follow in the footsteps of Jesus towards the new
millennium, as the rattle of gunfire carries from shore:
wobbling across a wrinkled brown sea rank with salt,
each step uncertain enough to be an act of faith.

Sunrise, San Francisco, September 1, 1999

"...As the clever hopes expire
Of a low dishonest decade..."
—W. H. Auden, "September 1, 1939"

Here on the piers along the Embarcadero,
looking east to where the lights of Oakland
dim and vanish in the fog, we huddle together
on a wet bench, waiting for the mist to lift,
for a luminous pencil-thin line of light
to trace the jagged outline of the hills.

Holding you close, I'm surprised to think
of Auden's poem, sixty years old today,
another "low dishonest decade" gone,
a new millennium already looming.

The din of war is scarcely dimmer now;
the "error bred in the bone" dismays us still.

A metallic whine like an insect's
pierces the early morning quiet.
Not far from where we sit, a chopper
from the Naval Base on Treasure Island
hovers like a bee above shadowy waters,
bent on some errand we can only guess.
I hardly dare love you in such a world.

A new day sketches itself in around us,
swelling dawn's silhouettes with form and color.
The mist disperses as the burning arc of sun
lifts over the rim of night, beautiful and terrible,
a skirt of fire trailing a brilliant hem.

Morning Meditation

for Rebecca Lyon

Inscribed on the rising mist, the pines
are characters in some strange alphabet
I've long ago forgotten how to read—
each branch a brushstroke placed deliberately,
spelling out something I seem meant to know:
a reassurance, or a call to praise.

One clear note shimmers and uncurls from
the lip of a delicate bell, shaped like a bowl,
a tone containing many tones within it,
its sound both simple and complex at once.
We close our eyes and concentrate on silence,
aware—for the first time—of our own breathing.

The farthest birdsongs sharpen and draw near.
Then, suddenly, the stillness is disturbed:
a wounded sound, like a suture being torn
from the air itself. I open my eyes to look
and glimpse a chicken hawk climbing to sunlight,
hauling a flurry of wingbeats after it.

The Yellow House In Arles

"Between two such beings as he and I," Gaugin reflected, "a sort of struggle was brewing."
—Joseph A. Harriss, "Strange Bedfellows," in ***Smithsonian****, December, 2001*

Gaugin, in later years, described
Van Gogh when they shared
the house in Arles as *fou*—crazy—
telling anyone who would listen
how the distraught Dutchman
once ran half-naked and screaming
into the street after him, on a night
swarming with whirlpool stars.

That was also the night Vincent
amputated his ear with a razor,
presenting the grisly trophy
to a girl in the local brothel.

His 1888 rendering of the yellow house
with the scalloped fanlight over its green door
betrays the maelstrom raging within—
where Gaugin complained his friend
had reduced their life to perpetual squalor.

The walls are executed with frenzied brushstrokes;
we can almost feel the roughness of their stucco.
But it's the sky above that demands our attention:
deep cobalt blue, neither day nor truly night—
an empty sky: starless, Godless, utterly hopeless.

Elegy Which Should Have Been A Blues

John Lee Hooker, 1917-2001

I met you years ago before a show,
waiting respectfully while you stood talking
to a young woman whose name was also Hooker,
who hailed from Mississippi as you did
and wondered whether you might be related.

Your speaking voice had in it all the grit
and anguish I'd admired on your records,
but there was an enormous dignity
about you no recording could convey.

By then you were a legend; even so,
when that young stranger introduced herself
you shook her hand and offered your own name,
as I imagined you'd been taught to do
when you were a child in the rural South.

In Response To A Prediction Of My Death On April 4, 2031

"What instruments we have agree:
The day of his death was a dark, cold day."
—W. H. Auden

A night just like tonight, perhaps; no moon,
only a few sullen clouds drifting languidly
towards the indifferent blister of the sunset,
the lights below them like embers in a fire.

I'll slip unnoticed from my wasted life,
the way a swimmer might discard a robe;
leaving behind me some few grieving friends;
sure, as I breathe my last, that I've been loved.

Should anyone miss me, let it be my wife;
and yet I'll leave the world with no regrets,
sure that the bond we share will last beyond
the narrow confines of our birth and death.

Then everything I was or might have been
will vanish into the realm of speculation:
nothing remaining of me but memories,
and some poetry no one will ever read.

A night just like tonight, or any other:
only a few dull clouds dispersing here
among the smoky tatters of the sky,
the city lights dissolving, and no stars.

Who Wants To Be An Impoverished Poet?

Should you decide to devote your life to poetry,
you would most likely become which of the following?

Is it:

A. Famous, and wealthy beyond all dreams of avarice;
B. Known and respected among scholars and academics;
C. Broke and obscure, in a room that leaks when it rains, or;
D. Dead before you reach the age of fifty?

Well, Regis, that would have to be A, wouldn't it?

Is that your final answer?

Part 3: The Ordinary Arrival of Death

Electrocuting The Elephant

Lulu's gone mad, but stubbornly refuses
to eat the poisoned carrots her keepers
have attempted to feed her; thus, another
means of dispatching her must be found.

It's 1904, a time when both
electrocution and moving pictures
are relatively recent developments
and very much novelties,
so the execution is preserved
in grainy black and white.

The great beast kneels
on the floor of her cage
in the first throes of mute
uncomprehending agony
as the labyrinth of wires
crossing her broad back
crackles with the current—
searing her skin, spitting sparks
into the forest of coarse hair
along the ridge of her spine.
Seconds later, her dark bulk
topples, the life gone out of it.

Macabre as it seems, this grisly
event is destined to become
a popular feature in early cinemas.
The film is silent, of course.
In the background, the lights
of Coney Island flicker
like candles in a rising wind.

The Ordinary Arrival Of Death

In memoriam: Marty Gordon

Cloudless sky, light like water on the street.

I'm depositing a check in an automatic teller when he
comes up behind me, grinning, removing his sunglasses,
amused by the lack of recognition, at first, in my eyes.

He stands smiling in the sun, handsome, young,
a shock of blond hair glowing on his forehead,
his face friendly, glad we've met—it's been years.
What do we talk about? An upcoming concert,
nothing much. "Nice to run into you again."

Later that night he's dead, fallen two stories
from an apartment balcony. Forgetting his key,
trying to climb in through a window, maybe drunk,
he lost his footing. I picture him grasping
at nothingness, spread on the air for an instant
as if in flight. And then darkness, nothing at all.

Droppings

"My God! If I'm stuck in Oakland much longer, I'll wind up writing poems about pigeon shit!"
—conversation with a friend

In an empty city where enormous
buildings blacken a thin lavender sky,
great clouds of pigeons fill the bare
winter trees like feathered foliage,
a dark mass trembling with its own
breeze even on nights of no wind.

Sometimes, as though in response
to some silent signal, hundreds
rise together in shattered spirals,
a debris of oily feathers trailing behind;
as a burnt moon climbs through clouds,
their cooing blankets the sidewalks like a moan.

And sometimes, the strangest things
are suddenly—inexplicably—beautiful.
Beneath the pigeon trees, spattered droppings
shine on the asphalt in the failing light.

The Dolls

On Sutter Street, a row of Barbie dolls
is posed in sidewalk-level windows.
The old kind with real lashes blooming above
the perpetual astonishment in their eyes.
Their clothing is anything but innocent.
Studded leather, suggestive lingerie.
Ken sports a gold jumpsuit, clutches
a Gay Pride flag. A Black Barbie
strokes a ceramic kitten, an enormous
indolent tiger beneath her tiny hand.

It's a land of vixens and beasts. Each evening
I see them on my way home, speculate
about who collected them, arranged them
so lovingly on a dusty windowsill.
Then one night they're gone, the apartment
dark and empty. Painters' ladders and drop cloths
dimly visible through the glass.

A Street At The End Of The World

On the next corner, a forlorn little man
in a shabby Salvation Army uniform
plays the trumpet, a few coins shining dully
in his open case, like wishes in a fountain
long since gone dry. You're walking along alone,
stepping carefully over an iron grating where
the bad breath of the unseen subway rises
in a blur of heated steam. Ahead of you,
a crowd has gathered around a wooden crate
where a hustler deals cards.

And then it happens:
suddenly, and without warning, as you watch
his agile hands, you find you're thinking again
how flesh would burn free of the bone in seconds,
hustler and onlookers vaporized,
the street consumed in a roaring wall of flames.

And on a day just like today, perhaps:
the last sky you will ever see—this sky—
blue as a china plate about to break.

Fourteenth Street, Greenwich Village, 1984

Watching The Tall Ships

for George R. Laurence

The wrinkled Hudson far below us held
only the cobalt of the cloudless sky
and scattered fragments of midsummer light.
The breeze that stirred the trees around us made
the water's surface too rough for reflections;
but even so, the shadows of the sails
swelled and grew full upon the moving river.

Off to the east, the spires of Manhattan
rose gray and stony through the soot and smog;
the masts that swayed against their grimness seemed
like a young forest growing on the slopes
of jagged mountains, sheltered from the weather.

We'd made our camp atop the Palisades
the night before, and risen before dawn
to stake our claim to this bald bit of rock:
a windswept granite outcropping which gave
an unobstructed view down river, towards
the harbor, towards the Verrazano Narrows
where the suspension bridge embraced the air
like a dull filament against the void.

George woke me earlier than I'd have liked.
Still groggy from a night of serious drinking,
we shaded our eyes and scanned the scene below;
the fierce glare from the water plunged its knives
into our brains, ripping our thoughts to shreds.

Now, the barque *Eagle* led the grand parade;
a swarm of smaller craft played in its wake,
while other tall ships slid in silhouette
beneath the bridge: schooners and Yankee clippers,
frigates, and whaling boats right out of Melville.
There must have been a hundred ships or more,
advancing with the splendor of a vision.

It was the summer before we left for college.
As always, George stood grinning at my side,
his boyish face flushed with enthusiasm,
his ginger hair already tinged with gray;
this was the summit of our innocence,
one fleeting moment when the future spread
before us like an endless possibility.

The years have run like water through my hands.
To say the world seemed *newer* then is wrong;
but when I think about that perfect dawn
high on the cliffs, it almost seems as though
I've lost the eye I once had for details.
Each line pulled taut against the shimmering sky,
each pole and spar, is burned into my mind
with a precision nothing since can match.

Einstein The Watchmaker

"If only I had known, I would have become a watchmaker."
—Albert Einstein, on his role in helping develop the atom bomb, 1955 (as quoted in ***Newsweek****)*

His wild hair brilliant by lamplight,
he squints through thick crystal
at the paper-thin gears his steady
hands place in their appointed
rounds, a well-ordered universe
being assembled on a tabletop.

It is already late. The tweezers
shine in his fingers like threads
of starlight. On nights like this,
he senses his destiny has always
had something to do with time,
although he sometimes wonders

whether it's really confined to
this tiny shop with its glittering
piles of stopped watches, its
ornate wooden cuckoo clocks
announcing each lonely hour
in a cacophony of song. It's

1955. The American invasion
of the Japanese mainland has
just ended, and with it, the last
vestige of the Second World War.
He is at peace tonight, except
for the recurring dreams which

have lately troubled him. Nightly, he sees
the world cleansed by a fire more horrible
than the fire of Malachi, millions of lives
vaporized in an instant. And at the boiling
center of the maelstrom, a voice repeating
gibberish, over and over: $E=MC^2$, $E=MC^2$…

Cockatoo And Cockroaches

for Victor Buxbaum

Grotesque as it seems, *Pet World*,
specializing in rare and unusual imports,
stocks a terrarium of Brazilian cockroaches
for the discriminating collector, shiny brown
wedges of life burrowing and scurrying
behind glass, flexing translucent wings.

There's also a cockatoo large as a cat,
brilliantly plumed in blue and gold,
but with a voice like something
in excruciating pain. It perches
on a swing in its huge cage, calmly
devouring the sign warning customers
not to get too close; repeated entreaties
produce nothing resembling human speech,
only a sort of sardonic chuckle
which sends a shiver through the afternoon.

Maxfield Parrish

see especially "Daybreak" (1922)

He plumbed a past of his own making,
choosing for self-portrait the Pied Piper;
enchanting us all with luminous skies
piled high with magnificent clouds.

Yet he was modern, painting mostly
for calendars and advertisements,
a medievalist in an age
of mass production.

As the twenties roared around him
he must have endured their emptiness,
yearning for a time before skyscrapers,
telephones, motor-cars and aeroplanes.

You know his most famous print:
two young boys loiter in vined darkness
after a swim; one bends over his companion,
tempting him into the water behind them.

Beyond the shadowed colonnade
jagged hills glow with fantastic light;
the blue world bleeds gently to brown;
no sound disturbs the early morning quiet.

The lake is burnished bronze:
so still and starless it seems to hold,
like an echo or the end of a dream,
the image of the departed night sky.

The Squirrels

for Bob and Kathy De Luccia

As we lay sleepless, we could hear them gnawing
above us, in the attic unused for years.
Traps did no good: sprung at the oddest hours,
and always empty whenever we went to look.

At first, we just used salted peanuts for bait;
then almonds, walnuts, currants, and finally
dried figs as round and rich as silver dollars.
But nothing worked, and so the noise continued.

When spring came, they were noisier than ever,
their small sounds mingled with the dripping eaves;
all day their elusive scurrying dogged us like
the nagging memory of a childhood song.

We gave them names, beginning to suppose
we could distinguish the movements of each one
from among so many furtive rustlings, hearing
sounds faint enough to have been our imagination.

Then, more and more, we started to believe
that they resembled us, their features and habits
not so dissimilar from our own, although in fact
we'd never so much as caught a glimpse of them.

And when the wind was howling through the pipes
we knew the squirrels were talking to their dead.
One summer night we finally found one; mangled,
it had fallen down our chimney and broken its neck.

We grieved as we might have for a relative,
held a backyard funeral for the tiny corpse
with all the usual pomp and circumstance.
The others chattered overhead like ghosts.

For Geoffrey Hill

> *"I will consider the outnumbering dead:*
> *For they are the husks of what was rich seed."*
> *—G. H., "Merlin," from* **For The Unfallen** *(1959)*

When the dead in Hell
gather together to drink
at their trough of blood
like flies at the throat
of a slaughtered bull,
their souls will be less
than the stench in the air,
their blathering blurred
to an inarticulate whine.

Your voice alone in that chorus of ghosts
will sing in finely-wrought, still-human tones:
witnessing how, in a century seduced by death,
the rigors of language imposed a conscience
on the lubricious world, almost subduing
for a moment the obscenity of history.

The Day They Closed The Mustang Ranch

"Sometime this summer, a bulldozer is supposed to slam into the nation's first legal whorehouse."
—***San Francisco Chronicle***, *April 23, 2003*

The low stuccoed building
broods in the desert sun.

At the cyclone fence by the main gate,
truckers from the interstate are turned away.

Sagebrush and memories remain;
miles of lonely Nevada highway.

A few of the girls linger in the parking lot,
in tight sequined dresses and short skirts,
their coats pulled close against a bitter wind.

No light penetrates the black-walled Dungeon Room,
where an enormous X sporting eyelets for chains
stands empty, its shackles dangling—
a vacant Cross awaiting a Savior.

Snow On The Colorado Plains

This late in the year a sudden thaw
seems to take the land by surprise:
the high, thin sky is achingly blue,
the weather so mild it could be
April instead of December.

But in places the shorn pastures
wear patches of unmelted snow,
where a tree's shadow or a boulder,
a stone wall or an abandoned barn,
has shielded the earth from sunlight.

Dulled to sepia by the dusty prairie wind,
these icy spots resemble the cloud shadows
one sometimes finds in old photographs;
they punctuate the surrounding landscape
like ominous pauses in conversation.

The Songwriter Addresses His Fans

"Prior to this lifetime
I surely was a tailor."
—Paul Simon, "Fakin' It," from ***Bookends*** *(1968)*

His dark, intelligent eyes are shaded
by the brim of a Yankees cap he pushes
back only once, revealing for an instant
a head grown nearly bald.

Pale and small, he's almost a caricature,
the cadence of Queens still in his speech:
an aging tailor or grocer, whose hands
seem to cry *oy vey!* with every gesture.

Then he begins to sing. An instrumental track
pours pure exuberance from concealed speakers;
his voice is strong as he adds the unfinished lyric.

He seems to swell in stature as he sings;
and for a moment, he grows young.

Bell Choir

In the chancel
silver bells flare in the sun,
lips upward, like chalices.
When they're shaken
clear notes spill
from them like water.
Only music makes the world
bearable—music, and sometimes love.
Melody washes over us now
as we drink deeply
from the invisible
wine of gratitude.

A Cyanide Lake In An Old Mining Town

Victor, Colorado

Its blue more faded than the frozen sky,
the water is the color of an eye—
blind and unblinking among the talus mounds,
it broods above the freight yards outside town:
too perfectly round for anyone to mistake
for either a sink-hole or a natural lake,
sheltered by slag heaps from the winter wind.

Here in the mountains, where the air is thinned,
the weak December sunlight seems to drain
down through the gravel filters like old rain—
as though the poisoned waters could extract
this metaphorical gold, as they in fact
once drew the true gold from the rock and rubble
back when the exhausted mine seemed worth the trouble.

Expulsion From The Garden

Porcelain plate, Italian, Urbino, mid 16th century

Once we were tenants of a fragrant Eden.
The world was new, both beautiful and terrible.
We were consumed by the terror and the glory,
like moths drawn near an incinerating flame
whose wings are charred until they match the darkness.

Who could have been content? We were invisible,
hidden in shadows we ourselves had cast:
the scant light of our lives was like the moon's
reflected glory, leaving us to doubt
whether the rumors we had heard were true
about a blazing radiance called *the sun.*

Now we wake to sunlight, blinking dumbly,
rubbing the sleep from eyes no longer blind,
and seeing the world at last for what it is:
not paradise, perhaps, but *ours*, and home.

At Your Bedside

for Pat, comatose following a hemorrhaged brain tumor

For more than four months now,
I have kept my bedside vigil, loving you,
fearing the world may prove unkind.

Your face is beautiful in sleep:
a placid mask beneath which
the dreams of your illness
lie gathered like embers—
a low, white heat unstirred
by morning's hand.

In The Shadow Of The Reaper

Site of the siege of Chartres, 1568

Beyond the walls, the failing light
falls on shorn fields lying fallow
in the husk of harvest, whispering
this emptiness was once an open grave.

Here, the bodies of the fallen festered,
stilled blood blackening their twisted limbs.
Beneath a ravenous cloud of flies, dead eyes
stared heavenward from splintered skulls.

Nothing remains of those heaped corpses now,
of the botched sacrifice's indecent meat:
the dull worm fattens on that glutted dust,
the bones have blurred into oblivion.

Flamingoes In The Camargue

Having expected beauty,
a conflagration of plumage
igniting the sullen afternoon,
you're surprised by how ugly
they really are, how ordinary.

They rise in a dusty cloud,
faded feathers tinged with pink,
like cotton used to dress a wound.

There is nothing graceful
about their ungainly flight.

The dark water trembles,
but offers no reflection
of their passage.

Peppermint Pig

At first glance, it appears
to be blown glass, or glazed
ceramic, a tiny figurine
so perfectly smooth
light drips off it like water.
The faintly pungent scent
of mint betrays it as candy,
its astonishing pink too hard
for the teeth. In certain families,
at Christmas, the peppermint pig
is broken for luck, shattered
by a blow from a hammer,
sweet fragments dissolving
like dreams on the tongue.
That's the way of it: luck,
when it finds us, arrives
in pieces, and we sift
through the rubble,
taking what we can.

Author Photo: Janet Wildung

Robert Lavett Smith was born in Michigan in 1957, and grew up in northern New Jersey, just outside New York City. He received a B.A. in French from Oberlin College in 1980; while a student there, he also studied creative writing with Stuart Friebert and David Young.

After graduating from Oberlin, he went on to receive an M.A. in English with an emphasis in writing from the University of New Hampshire, where he studied with Charles Simic and Mekeel McBride. During the Fall of 1982, he was a member of the Master Class of the 92nd Street Y in New York, and studied with Galway Kinnell. In 1987, he moved to San Francisco, where he met his wife, Pat.

He has survived a wide variety of jobs over the past twenty years, and currently works as a Special Education Paraprofessional at George Washington High School in the Richmond district.

In addition to this, his first full-length collection, he is the author of four small-press chapbooks, and has published poetry in more than fifty literary magazines.

www.ingramcontent.com/pod-product-compliance
Lightning Source LLC
LaVergne TN
LVHW091206080426
835509LV00006B/858

* 9 7 8 0 9 7 6 1 9 5 4 2 9 *